Choosing a
Dressage
Horse

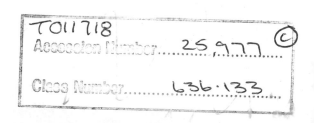

Choosing a Dressage Horse

LÉONIE M. MARSHALL

J. A. Allen
London

British Library Cataloguing-in-Publication Data.
A catalogue record for this book is available from the British Library

ISBN 0.85131.634.4

Published in Great Britain in 1996 by
J. A. Allen & Company Limited,
1 Lower Grosvenor Place, Buckingham Palace Road,
London, SW1W 0EL

Typeset by Textype Typesetters, Cambridge
Printed by Dah Hua Printing Press Co., Hong Kong

Illustrations by Maggie Raynor
Designed by Judy Linard
Text photographs by Bob Langrish
Cover photograph by Elizabeth Furth

Contents

List of Photographs

List of Illustrations

Introduction

Looking back at some of the horses with which I have been involved over the years, I find that the ones who were the most successful I had foisted on me for one reason or another, and were not particularly what I would have chosen.

For example, my first dressage horse was a swap for a horse I had been trying to event, but who turned out to be unrelentingly careless. Someone else thought they would try their chances (without success) and I acquired Oberon, a French thoroughbred bought at the Ascot bloodstock sales. He was small, only 15.3 hh with distinct limits to his stride, but he had a nice nature, good enough conformation to be a hack, and in spite of a huge buck, which he once threw in coming up a centre line, he made international status.

Another of my horses, an ex-racehorse who had steeplechased successfully, was a gift, because he had broken down and been fired. His owner did not want him to go on the open market and preferred to give him away. I remember his arrival; he came off the lorry like a dragon, breathing fire, his body gleaming with sinewy muscle. I wondered what I had taken on, especially as I soon discovered that he only wanted to canter on the near fore and could not cope at all without a strong hold on the bit, preferably with his tongue over it! Eventually he competed successfully in advanced classes and was placed in two international competitions in this country.

Othello was a rogue. He was given to me in the hope that

I could do something with him; he had been everywhere else and his next stop was the meat man! He was the most difficult horse I have ever had and many times I nearly shot him myself, but he taught me more than any other horse and was the most successful for me both here and abroad.

Unquestionably, it is a difficult job to choose the right horse, even given unlimited finance. Sometimes it can be worthwhile trying to make the most of what you have or what you can afford, rather than embarking on an endless and expensive search for the ideal horse. The more you look, the more you realise that perfection is more of a desire than a practicality. All horses have something wrong with them, even if it is only their colour or sex. Naturally the nearer to perfection we can get the better because it makes life easier, but there are ways of improving your horse by feeding, training or disguising faults by clever technique that will help to overcome his shortcomings.

I have written this book to try to give some hope and incentive to anyone interested in dressage whose horse has problems of conformation, mind, temperament, age or gait. I have attempted to cover the many problems we all encounter and have given some suggestions as to how to tackle them.

1
The Dressage Type

Before going on to specific points relating to choice, I would like to spend a short time discussing the various types and breeds with which we can be involved.

The Lippizaner: a breed that epitomizes the classical school of horsemanship.

Ponies

Without wishing to offend anybody, I have found that the chief difficulty in training ponies for dressage is their young riders. This is not to decry their ability but, because of their age they lack seat and leg, and experience.

A knowledgeable adult can do quite a lot to help, especially if they are small enough to ride the pony, and, if they are not, work on long reins or on the lunge with side-reins can at least teach the pony to go in a round outline with activity, and some acceptance of the bit.

A pony with extravagant movement will be difficult for the average child to sit on and will need to be made very supple to keep his back 'soft'. Children may well have to be trained to become secure in the saddle by being taught on a safe lunge-pony with or without reins and/or stirrups.

As their seat develops, their feel for what is happening underneath them will also develop, they will then be able to tell when the pony is going forwards correctly, whether or not he is in a rhythm, and if he is keeping a nice outline.

One advantage children have is that, on the whole, they are very receptive and can be taught to ride to orders, which will be necessary if they are to compete successfully.

Concentration can be a problem, but if they are not expected to work for very long periods to begin with, and, as their conception of what is required improves, the desire to do well will aid concentration.

I have found that any child, interested in schooling, will, from the age of about ten, be able to understand and ride all school exercises up to medium standard, and some will be able to teach their ponies flying changes as time goes on.

However capable the children become, there will probably be additional problems with the ponies. The problem of stride, or lack of it, is one of the most difficult. The average pony will probably have very little length of stride and almost no suspension between the steps or strides. I know from trying to judge ponies how fast their legs seem to go as they bustle round the arena.

It is very difficult to get some ponies going and it is dispiriting for a young child to try to ride tests on these ponies. They may be able to achieve a reasonable standard just to ride a Pony Club Horse Trials dressage test, but it may be expecting too much of them to go further in dressage. Fortunately, lazy ponies are generally ridden by very young children who are probably not going to ride dressage tests anyway.

I do think children should learn to use a whip correctly and effectively (under supervision) quite early so that they do not have to flail their legs continuously. Ponies seldom respond satisfactorily to flapping legs and I feel that it is never too soon for children to try to learn to ride in a way that will be helpful to them as adult riders. Riding dressage is difficult enough without having to learn one thing as a child and then having to change later.

Ponies who bustle around generally lack rhythm in their gaits and do need riding more steadily in order to find any kind of regularity of step. Children should be encouraged to count to themselves in order to keep the steps regular. The trot can be improved vastly by having a rhythm and so, of course, can the canter, but the latter is generally more difficult as a certain amount of strength is required from the rider to help balance the pony. I think that teaching a pony to canter on the lunge so that he can learn to go slowly and steadily by himself is a great help.

Ponies are not often chosen specifically for dressage because they are generally required for other aspects of riding as well, but if you were setting out to choose one for the job he would require exactly the same qualities as a horse: good action, temperament and appearance.

With this in mind, prospective purchasers should not be swayed by any particular breed, although some of the native breeds are not really suitable. An excellent specimen of a breed may well have the qualities that make him a champion but would nevertheless render him unsuitable for dressage. I refer to the limited gaits which some of the smaller native ponies possess, and to their width which

15

Mornington Crescent, a good type of pony for dressage.

certainly does not assist young riders to get their legs around the pony.

Neither can it be said that the bigger native ponies are more suitable because, although they may have a more extravagant action, this can often be too rounded and high, causing a problem for young people when trying to sit in trot for example.

Native crosses are often a good choice, but, as with all breeding, nothing is ever guaranteed and a winner is sometimes found in the most unlikely places.

Cobs

These often delightful and useful creatures have varied breeding. There are of course the Welsh cobs, the section Cs and Ds who maintain a very distinct type in build and action. Their main problem with regard to dressage is that they are a bit small, the Cs being smaller than the Ds, but even these seldom make over 15.2 hh. They tend to be full of go, and may have quicksilver temperaments. Their action is flamboyant with tremendous flexion of the hind leg joints, a lot of shoulder lift, and an extravagant rounded action of the front legs.

They can make very good riding horses and do well in dressage, but, although they have the ability, because of their size, cobs would not be bought by ambitious dressage riders. However, some of the most successful dressage horses have been Welsh crosses.

Other than the Welsh Section Cs and Ds, the cob is a specific type resulting from the crossing of various equine types. Some are heavier in build than others, and size varies enormously. They are nearly all a good shape, although some may be short of neck, and most of them have good temperaments.

A hairy cob can, amongst his other duties as an all-round family horse, perform well, and provide fun, at the lower levels of dressage.

17

I have had a variety of cobs to train; some move very adequately for dressage, and others have been disappointingly limited in their stride.

I would always give a cob a second look, but would be more enthusiastic about a crossbred with a 'round' outline and good active action. Finding a good cob-cross is quite difficult and, they are, today, quite expensive, because they are so often bought for hunting, jumping or showing.

Thoroughbreds

I have always loved the Thoroughbred, both to look at and to teach, because they learn so easily. This is a great attribute providing they learn the correct thing! In spite of this personal preference I have to say that, on the whole, they are not really all that suitable as dressage horses.

A Thoroughbred (Secretariat).

I believe there are two stumbling blocks. Firstly, their build; the Thoroughbred, although beautiful, often lacks strength in the back and hindquarters where much of the strain is taken when trying to achieve great collection and impulsion. Secondly, being highly strung, many Thoroughbreds cannot take the pressure of training. Having been bred for galloping, they find the restrictions of an arena and the necessary demands of control too much to cope with. They may react by becoming 'hot' as they try to evade their rider's aids, or they may nap to avoid what is difficult.

Riders should train Thoroughbreds with great sympathy and understanding, and a knowledge of how to build the work up gradually in order to strengthen the muscles required for dressage. A lot of patience will be needed to give the Thoroughbred time to mature physically and mentally. There is a great temptation to rush the training before there is sufficient strength because they learn so quickly.

I believe young Thoroughbreds need longer periods of free, forward riding compared to a Warmblood horse of the same age who can start work in the school straight away.

I would not turn away a Thoroughbred but would prefer to train one with the stamp of a steeplechaser rather than that of a flat-race horse, providing it was not too tall and rangy. The Thoroughbred bred for flat racing generally tends to be too light in bone and substance and can have a rather 'spikey' action. They can also look rather small and insignificant in the arena.

Arabs

There are many Arab horse enthusiasts in this country but, strangely, few seem to bother training them for even moderate dressage. In fact, I believe that the Arab is sometimes maligned as a stupid animal, only suitable for parading his beauty in in-hand or show classes. Far from being stupid, I would say that his problem is that he is

19

brighter than most riders, working out ways to do as he wishes in spite of them!

I have often been irritated by some Arab habits. For instance, they naturally like to go along with their heads in the air and probably their tails too! This leads to hollowness of the back, and the hocks working behind the quarters in a thrusting action.

In trot they sometimes have very 'flat' steps, with almost no suspension, and in canter appear stiff-legged or stilted and frequently change legs behind to balance.

The fact that they have one less rib than other horses I do not believe is of great significance as regards training, but the high build of the croup has as it makes it very difficult to obtain a lowering of the hindquarters.

Despite these difficulties, it has been proved that the Arab can be trained to quite a high standard of dressage if systematic training is used to achieve a round outline, and if

An Anglo-Arab, ridden by Diana Mason.

there is a willing acceptance of aids many of the physical faults are overcome or disguised. They can also become willing partners in the training procedure if riders treat them as horses and not simply as an adornment.

In addition to the Arab, there are the Anglo Arabs and part-bred Arabs, many of whom are as good or better than any other type of horse, having some of the Arab beauty but gaining size and substance from whatever the Arab blood was crossed with.

Warmbloods

I suppose most people who want to go to the top in dressage would buy a Warmblood horse given the finance; the reputation they have for winning competitions makes them an obvious choice. They do possess many attributes.

A Hannoverian (Demonstrator), ridden by Ferdi Eilberg

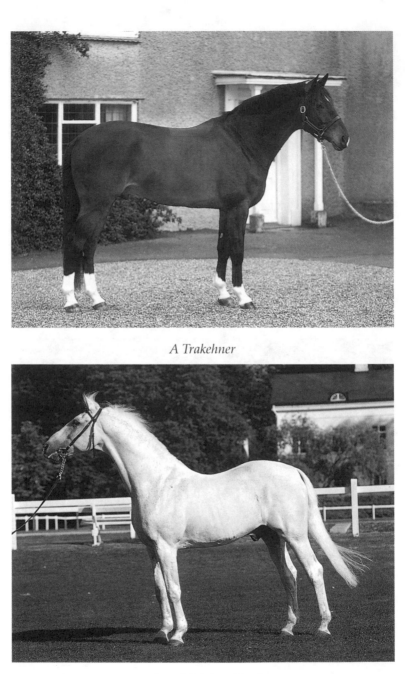

A Trakehner

A Swedish Warmblood.

Most are impressive with good substance, bone and, often, height. They stand out like giants amongst mice.

Their shape has much to recommend it because the way they have been bred over the years has produced a consistant shape which becomes easily rounded, when ridden onto the aids.

Stride of course is a big factor. Some of these horses are more spectacular than others, but all, almost without exception, have built-in suspension and rhythm.

They also have a very equable nature, and are unruffled by the sometimes severe demands of training. They may be a bit slow to grasp an exercise occasionally, but will not be put into a flap by something being repeated many times. This attitude can sometimes be a problem for the rider because if they are too 'laid-back' mentally, then they may also be very idle and thick-skinned, consequently the aids of the rider need to be strong and effective.

I think riders, particularly female, should be warned about the danger of buying something too big. It is always a mistake to be over-horsed, but especially so with a Warmblood. If he is not idle, he will have the kind of power that is too much for the average rider to control. If he is lazy, it will be a perpetual and exhausting struggle.

In Europe, where the Warmblood originated, many of the lady riders have male trainers to set the horses up for them and although times are changing, nearly all European riders, male and female, will have more knowledge of training that type of horse than we have in Britain.

Other Crossbreds

There are so many other types that is is impossible to pinpoint any one in particular, although I suppose one of the most popular would be the Thoroughbred-cross. The non-Thoroughbred half of the cross can be anything from Arabs to Shires, so the variation in build, size, stride and temperament is enormous.

23

Presence and General Conformation

Whatever the breeding, the really important thing to assess when looking at a potential dressage horse is, first, does he strike you as something special? Will he stand out in a huge class of novices and will he gain the judge's attention? Later this distinctive quality should give his training a veneer of 'class' which will make him recognisable in the future.

The second important factor is the conformation. Ask yourself whether the animal matches front and back, in other words, is he in balance? A horse with a massive forehand which tails off behind the saddle will never look good, nor will he be able to work well. Similarly, it is no use having a powerful rear end and a forehand short of shoulder or neck.

The length of the horse is also important; problems can be caused if he is either too long or too short in the back. The rider should sit in the centre of the horse to look right, so a very long-backed horse would have too much behind the rider and a very short-backed one could make the rider look too tall.

Ideally there should be an in-built arch to the crest rising from the withers. The head should fit onto the neck in a way which allows the poll to bend easily, and there should be no thickness where neck and head meet underneath.

Limbs need to be strong and four-square, taking equal weight, with good rounded feet; their size being relevant to the stature of the horse.

I prefer a wide horse to a very narrow one because the latter tends to look like a razor blade coming up the centre line.

A horse's action is, of course, important and, although we all love to see something extravagant, and it is an asset to a dressage prospect, a horse with this type of action is not necessarily the easiest or best to train. However, a rounded action of the front legs is easier to cope with than a straight action, and, similarly, a good bending action of the hind legs will make a horse look as if he is working hard.

Natural extension obviously cuts out a tremendous amount of work, but I have known many horses who have, miraculously it seems, learnt to extend after several years work.

I have found that a bad canter is one of the hardest things to improve and, in order to see what sort of natural moment of suspension the horse possesses, I ask the vendor to turn him loose in a suitable area to show off his gaits unhindered. A bad walk can also be a real bugbear but I might ignore this and hope to make an adequate improvement.

2
A Trained Horse

Many people buy schoolmasters (older horses with a good training, but who are past their best for competition) or, more ambitiously, horses which have the potential to go to the top and already know all the Grand Prix work.

Nearly all these horses come from abroad having been trained, almost exclusively, by continental trainers; the advantage being that the horses will have been well-drilled in their routines and will, to a degree, be able to help their new riders, at least for a time. Nevertheless, however well a horse is trained he cannot possibly retain the quality of his work by himself if the rider does not have the experience. If the new owner has a knowledgeable trainer, the work can be retained, but there are few of these trainers available.

I think it is very sad indeed to see a willing well-trained horse being badly ridden. So often the horse is desperately trying to do that which he knows he has to do, having been given an aid of sorts, but then being totally hindered in the execution. If this goes on for too long the training and the competition marks will gradually slip away.

Again, one of the main problems with buying a schoolmaster, if you are female, is size, because many schoolmasters are Warmbloods and, as I have stated, Warmbloods tend to be big and have been trained by men. There are very few women who can ride with the control of a man simply because they do not have the same strength.

There is no doubt in my mind that if it is possible to train your own horse, having found a suitable one, this is the best way to success. Not only do you learn how to ride him, because you have taught him and overcome the countless problems on the way, but also because that all-important rapport which makes a partnership, is hard to establish without a well-founded marriage between horse and rider.

3
Untrained Horses

Sometimes, for financial reasons or simply for preference, you may choose a young horse. If you decide to have a foal and start right at the beginning, then you will almost certainly know the breed you want before looking around. The breed would determine, at least approximately, the height, weight and possible action you could expect when the young horse matures.

One of the main difficulties with acquiring a youngster is that you will not know what the horse's temperament will be; an equable foal roaming happily in the field with his mother or friends will not necessarily display the same even temper when he is ultimately ridden and schooled, but that is one of the risks you take. Naturally, most youngsters inherit their temperament from the parents, so to lessen this risk, acquaint yourself with the sire and dam if possible.

If you have studied conformation, it will be possible to see whether the young foal conforms to the correct proportions. This may be more difficult to judge as he grows into a rather lanky yearling, possibly 'up at the back', when the front and hind ends grow at different rates. As a two- or three-year-old, the shape matures and he will fill out, showing more clearly how he will look when he has finished growing.

Most people (apart from those involved with racing and in-hand showing) will not do a great deal with their youngsters until they are three. At that age they will be strong enough to learn some basic discipline on the lunge and will probably also be 'backed' and ridden until they learn what the basic aids mean. After that some people turn them out until the start of their four-year-old year, when they will be reminded of their early lessons and then ridden on. If a horse is well-developed and mature in his three-year-old year, work may well be continued without the break which, if it is successful, gives him quite an advantage.

Although choosing a youngster and bringing it on yourself is not only fun but also an advantage from the point of view of not having any faults to eradicate, breaking and training a horse needs much knowledge and should not be undertaken by the uninitiated. Many a good horse can be spoilt by being broken badly.

If you are doubtful about your ability to do the job properly, it would be wise to set an amount of money aside so that you can send the horse to an expert for anything up to three months. The expert will then have time to not only break the horse but also to introduce him to many of the things he will meet later in life which will make him safer for you when he returns.

One word of warning: if you have not been taught how to lunge or long-rein do not experiment, because, if anything should go wrong, the expert who finally gets the job will have twice the trouble and it may end up costing more than you anticipated.

4
Size and Suitability

I think that there are two particular points to consider. First, the size of the rider should be suitable for the horse and vice versa. A very tiny person trying to wield a large horse round the restrictive size of an arena, is nearly always a disaster. The horse finds the arena awkward, tends to flounder round the corners, and becomes unbalanced. Unless the rider is exceptionally strong in the seat, he or she will be unable to help the horse, therefore a ragged performance is most likely.

Equally, if a rider is much too tall, too large or too heavy, he will hinder his horse's balance and action. Very heavy, cumbersome horses do tend to find school exercises and small arenas a bother. Purchasers should look for athleticism in their horses as well as being athletic themselves. Narrow horses with poor bone and small feet may find the work too hard. They make more fuss about heavy going and are generally unimpressive.

This brings me to my second point, i.e. the picture the horse will make in the arena. Naturally if the training is incorrect, even the most beautiful horse will not win, but the impression he makes in the judge's mind is all important for his future, so the better the picture, the greater his chances.

Once again, a huge horse labouring round under a weak rider will not create a good impression, nor will a small one with a lanky rider's legs dangling below his belly.

The matching of horse and rider will play a very big part in their future success.

5
Temperament

Excitable

A naturally excitable temperament can be difficult to cope with and these horses are often unsuitable for dressage. With calm riding, patience and sympathy, much can be achieved, but everything will take longer. Expecting these horses to learn quickly or calmly may bring disappointment. It will be necessary to take extreme care with every schooling session in order not to cause a problem by lack of thought or preparation, and everything must be taught slowly.

Excitable horses generally want to rush about so the first thing to teach them is to slow down; only then will they be receptive to learning. These horses tend to blackmail their riders by hotting up when they are brought onto the aids. However difficult it is for the rider, he must persist with the aids because there will be no hope of gaining control without them. They must of course be used sympathetically because, if the hands are used harshly or restrict the horse, and the legs do not hold the horse's sides calmly and quietly, this in itself would cause hotting up. If the rider is sure that his aids are satisfactory, then the horse must be made to become accustomed to them.

Other problems will be encountered because the excitable horse uses a variety of evasions to avoid control. He may tilt his head on one side, put his tongue over the bit, swing his quarters, jog and so on. All can be resolved by the

31

acceptance of the aids, but sometimes the battle seems endless, and consideration must be given to whether or not it is all worth the great effort involved.

Lazy

Like all idle creatures, including ourselves, the lazy horse will not really want to do anything. It can be most frustrating if a horse actually has the right conformation, looks and stride, and the ability to be great if only he would make the effort.

A great many horses can be shaken out of their slothfulness if the problem is tackled when they are youngsters. They must be taught that if they do not go forwards willingly from the rider's leg, they will get a sharp reminder from the schooling whip. Once they respect the leg they seldom bother to think of any evasions, and, consequently, become useful dressage horses. If this type of horse can be made fit enough to cope with the work, they also make very reliable competition horses, although possibly lacking the spark of a real champion.

Older, lazy horses are rather more of a problem. The equine species can be incredibly thick-skinned and become amazingly 'dead' to any use of legs, spurs or whips. I have ridden some unbelievably 'dead' horses who have switched off mentally, and become, apparently, totally unfeeling physically. I would certainly not bother to try to retrain, or even ride, such animals. It is very sad when this happens and should be a warning to those responsible for their training.

Nervous

Horses are timid by nature although there is a great variance in the timidity of foals. Some are inquisitive and will accept humans from the day they are born, while others will keep their distance. Even older youngsters who have not been handled from birth will become tame at different times and in different ways. Once they have become confident, it is our responsibility to maintain their trust, and not do anything which could cause them to fear us.

When training them we can easily make horses become nervous if we are too hard on them, expect too much too soon, punish them unreasonably, confuse them by inconsistant aids or ask them to do something they do not understand. They often show their anxiety by grinding their teeth or becoming tense which, providing the rider recognises the problem and sorts out the reason for it happening, will not continue to be a difficulty.

Nervous horses can be irritating because they seem to react unreasonably, but they only do so because they anticipate some unpleasant repercussion from the rider, so it is up to us to be patient and clear with our requests.

Unwilling

I have found that there is a small percentage of horses who appear to be unwilling or even nappy, from a very early age. They do not want to co-operate with humans and object by kicking, biting or refusing to move. Coercion may result in even more resentment and unless this can be overcome quickly, these horses will always be a nuisance. Some, sadly, perhaps never change, although others will learn to submit to human superiority.

Some may appear to give in, but having discovered that there are certain things they can get away with, will use this discovery to their own advantage, i.e. they may stop when they wish to dung, refuse to go passed objects, through water, or to keep up with other horses. When schooling these horses it may be difficult to supple them, to make them work on the aids or go forwards energetically. They are, in reality, only performing with about fifty per cent of their ability and are on the path to becoming really nappy.

The lazy ones will not take this nappiness very far, but the brighter ones will, over a period of time, become more conscious of their own desires and much less willing to respond to those of their riders.

It is probably true to say that there is a nap, or potential nap, in every horse and it will depend entirely on the reaction of the rider as to whether it develops or not. Although it is possible to retrain a nappy horse, it is a difficult and long job, requiring a good deal of knowledge and persistance, and is often not worth the bother unless you think the horse is exceptionally talented; even then they often have the last laugh, as I know to my cost.

6
Age

Dressage training does require a good deal of mental and physical agility, so the more receptive the horse's brain and the more supple his body the easier it will be. A young horse will be more likely to have these qualities and he will have the advantage of learning everything from scratch. All horses are born with a tendency to be one-sided, but a youngster's body will be devoid of the kind of stiffness and one-sidedness induced by bad riding.

If you buy him unbroken, then you will need considerable knowledge to teach him to lunge and long-rein and the understanding and nerve to back and ride him. People who know this process and can make a really good job of it are rare, and so, if you buy something already broken but subsequently hacked out and not schooled, you may find that the young horse already has decided some things for himself. A combination of tact and determination will then set you on the right path.

An older horse may well take longer to train than a young one because, although the latter will need time to develop physically, the older horse will almost surely have faults which need to be corrected, stiffness or habits which need eradicating, and all that can take years not months.

Something I think is quite remarkable is a horse's capacity for continuing to learn or relearn until they are at least twenty years old. They seem to have a greater ability than their riders, very often, to learn something new and are also prepared to do so.

7
Colour

This subject is a very personal one because we all have different preferences. If I saw a horse I liked which I thought could do the job I would not turn him down simply because I was not too keen on his colour.

There always used to be prejudice against broken-coloured horses, and I have yet to see one in Grand Prix, and it may have been because coloured horses seldom had the necessary qualities to go places in top class dressage because of mixed breeding. However, with the current increased interest in the type, which may lead to selective breeding, dressage arenas could in the future be graced by broken-coloured horses.

Whatever colour you choose, try to visualise it in an arena. Is it aesthetically pleasing, or does it distort the overall look? Is it going to attract the judge's eye or is he going to be astonished by some rather glaring markings? For example, white covering almost the whole head like a Hereford cow, or a great white splash on one side only, could be considered glaring. Similarly, extensively long stockings, especially if odd, can be unattractive, as can white splashes under the stomach.

On the other hand a certain amount of white draws the eye. A chestnut with four white stockings (equal if possible) and a blaze, providing it does not disappear over one nostril which can give the impression that the head tilts, would stand out.

A dark bay with socks on the hind legs and a star on the

forehead is always a good bet. Their coats can really shine and a dark colour stands out against the light background of an arena. Plain bays can be at a disadvantage unless they have plenty of presence.

Greys look nice when they are young and dappled but, I think, need to be quite big because the smaller ones, especially when white with age, can look insignificant.

When all is said and done, dressage is about training, but even so you want the picture you present to the judge to help sway him or her in your favour.

8
Gaits

Walk

SHORT-STRIDING

There are a large number of horses who have very short
strides in walk and they tend to step quickly to get along,
rather than stretching. This is usually due to poor
conformation but some get into a habit of walking this way
because it is less effort.

When buying a horse always look at him walking loose
in the field, on a lunge without side reins or, under the rider
on a free rein. You will then see the natural length of stride
the horse possesses. A horse should overtrack, i.e. the hind
feet should step over the prints made by the forefeet, but
there may be some horses whose natural conformation
does not allow them to do so. Horses vary enormously as
to how much they overtrack. Some will barely do so and
some will have a space of 12 inches between the fore and
back prints.

There are those horses who will not overtrack simply
because they are idle so some improvement can be made by
waking them up and making them walk out. Also, horses
who are used to going along with their heads in the air and
their backs hollow – perhaps because of bad training or
riding – seldom overtrack, but if they have the right
conformation a lot of improvement is generally possible
once they are schooled onto the bit and made to go in a
rounded outline.

Riders do sometimes inhibit their horses' walk, by trying to hurry them along instead of achieving a steady rhythm and then pushing the horse without losing the beat.

Riders who 'shovel' the horse along with their seats in the belief that this drives the horse forward are in fact generally impeding the action. The horse must be made to do the work, not the other way round. I have found that the walk generally improves when the rider sits quietly on the horse with relaxed seat muscles, absorbing the horse's natural movement, and then encouraging him with quiet, but firm, leg aids.

PACING
This term is used when horses walk with the legs on the same side coming forwards together, so that the appearance is of marching in two-time, instead of the steps being separated from each other making a four-beat gait. I have seen foals walk this way so it is sometimes a natural gait, although riders are often guilty of producing this type of walk if they hurry the stride and do not aim for a good regular rhythm. It can be difficult to prevent a horse from pacing and so a good assessment should be made when looking at the horse loose to see whether he tends to do this himself or whether it only occurs when he is ridden. I have found that the only way to prevent pacing in walk is to ride the gait slowly giving the horse more time to take a long step and move into a positive rhythm.

Personally I would prefer to try to improve the poor walk of a short-striding or idle horse than the pace because it is, on my opinion, unattractive and does lose a lot of marks in competition.

IRREGULAR
When looking at a prospective purchase you may notice something worrying about the horse's gait when he is ridden that is not apparent when he is loose. This would indicate that one of the horse's riders has allowed, or caused, a problem to creep in. This can be the case with an

irregular walk, which simply means that the beat of the steps is not a correct walk rhythm.

If you notice an irregularity when you ride the horse yourself, see whether you can achieve and maintain a true four-beat gait. It may be that all you have to do is to ride the walk more slowly, but it could be that the horse is not straight which can cause unevenness. Sometimes a mouth resistance will make the gait irregular, one side of the mouth being less sensitive than the other. Stiffness can also be the cause. Whatever the cause loosening the jaw and making the horse equally supple on both sides would normally help to make an improvement.

An irregularity could, at worst be caused by lameness but if you are having the horse vetted, you should mention the problem to the vet so that he can investigate for you before you purchase the horse.

Trot

ELEVATED
Natural elevation in the trot gait means that there is a noticeable period of suspension between the two diagnol pairs of legs. Some horses have more natural elevation than others. When both diagonals are even and equal this natural elevation gives the gait a rhythm and presence which can make it very attractive to watch. Generally this elevation is also associated with scope which means that the horse will be able to lift his shoulder upwards and forwards while the hind legs propel the hindquarters in a similar manner. This scope will enable the horse to vary his stride within the gait and most probably produce medium and extended trot easily.

There can be several problems attached to natural elevation. The first, and most often seen, is that the rider, feeling the precise rhythm which the horse holds so easily, will be fooled into thinking that he does not have to ride forwards energetically. Although the trot may look and feel quite nice, there will be a danger of the impulsion hovering, or dwelling, for a split second, causing hesitation where there should be positive energy taking the horse forwards. However, these horses do not have difficulty in maintaining a good rhythm even when ridden forwards more.

If they are not ridden well forward, the lack of impulsion will allow the elevation to lift the horse upwards instead of forwards into a sort of false passage. Generally this is accompanied by a stiffness in the back and a feeling that the horse is 'drawing back' from the bit instead of taking the bit and moving forwards.

The next problem may be that, in piaffe, the horse will find it difficult to shorten his steps because of his natural elevation. Providing he is taught to shorten his trot by means of half halts and not allowed to become croup high, the piaffe can be attained. He should always be kept well forward, 'in front' of the rider's leg and not allowed to drop impulsion or come off the aids.

As stated, *generally* elevation is associated with scope but there are a few horses who have a wonderful natural lift to their trot gait but who never seem to be able to alter the stride to produce extension. It can be very disappointing to discover that the trot you had thought was so spectacular does not have scope. This would show when the horse is trotting loose; another good reason for seeing the horse at liberty in the school or field.

A trot will often change when the rider first begins work, and can lose some of the stride you may have seen when the horse was loose. If, however, the stride is seen in the natural state, there is a strong chance it will return and, in any case, good extensions very often do not appear until the horse has been in systematic work for a while, during which time sufficient balance and impulsion have built up to give the gait maximum power.

SHORT STRIDING
Horses with a naturally short stride in trot will almost certainly be difficult to train for dressage because their lack

41

of scope will make it very difficult to obtain any real differences within the gait. Because the stride is limited, any attempt to make the horse lengthen will almost certainly result in hurrying.

If a good rhythm is developed, with a gradual build-up of impulsion, some difference in the gait may be satisfactorily achieved but will probably still only give the horse three gait variants (collection, working, medium) instead of four as required, the fourth being extension.

FLAT (LACKING SUSPENSION)

There are many horses who, when they trot, have a disappointingly flat trot lacking any real suspension between the diagonal pairs of legs. I would not choose a horse with such a trot because the gait is going to be limited in several respects.

First of all, because of the lack of lift, it will be difficult to make the horse cover the ground. In other words he will take many short steps to get where he is going because he cannot gain ground in the moment when one pair of diagonal legs has propelled him forwards and upwards, and before the other pair meet the ground.

Trying to teach passage to a horse with a flat trot causes a lot of difficulty and is possibly heartbreaking for the rider. The piaffe will be easier but there will still tend to be a lack of spring in the movement.

Obtaining a clear rhythm from a flat trot is sometimes difficult and, to the observer or judge, will create a poor impression of the gait, therefore marks are harder to come by. Making the horse work well on the aids in a rounded outline and by using lateral exercises to supple him will help a flat trot look more rhythmic, but trying to achieve real differences within the gait can be a long job although not an impossible one.

Systematic work, development of muscles and 'carrying power' from impulsion can do a lot to lift a horse with a flat trot into 'overdrive', but the question to ask yourself is, is it worth the effort?

If you already own a horse with a flat trot, you might not want to part with him, but if you are looking for a horse then I suggest you avoid buying one with this gait problem.

LONG-STRIDING

Clearly a horse with a good long stride would be preferable to one which takes short steps, because he will have plenty of scope to cover the ground. It is, however, important to assess or discover if the horse can shorten his stride when asked because this will be vital to collection. There are some horses who find it so difficult to shorten their steps that they would rather elevate and/or 'parade' with a stiff, straight front leg like a soldier in slow march. This is very tiresome because it takes a good deal of time and skill to teach the horse to shorten correctly. Most of the impulsion must be temporarily removed so that there is very little possibility of elevation and the horse must be kept soft in the mouth and supple in the back to avoid the 'parade' trot.

Teaching piaffe is beneficial to this correction, although, if it is taught early in the horse's training, it would be more of a training piaffe (stepping forwards) rather than the full piaffe for which he would not be ready.

As with any trot the moment of suspension needs to be clear.

The long-striding flat trot which some Thoroughbreds have can create its own problems because this combines the difficulties of the flat trot with the difficulty of having to shorten the stride. If there is virtually no suspension the horse cannot even elevate to try to achieve what his rider is asking. This can lead to the horse feeling trapped by his rider's demands and seeking ways to evade the problem.

Sitting on a horse with a long stride can be a wonderful feeling but the rider will need a secure seat and the ability to become part of the movement. It is quite easy to get left behind and end up making the horse go more slowly just to make it easier to sit on.

43

CLOSE IN FRONT

This can be quite a worry particularly if the horse continually knocks one fetlock with the opposite hoof, because he could end up permanently lame. Some horses knock their fetlocks because they do not move a particular foot forwards quite straight, but, on the whole, they do so because they are too narrow in the chest, and the legs are therefore too close together.

The problem can be overcome by always riding in brushing boots, but the rules of dressage competitions preclude any use of boots or bandages, and it is disastrous if the horse strikes and lames himself in the middle of a test.

CLOSE BEHIND

With correct conformation the horse will stand and move foursquare. There are, however, those who appear to stand correctly but, in action, move rather close at the back. As with being close in front, any damage done with one foot to an opposite fetlock or leg can be a disaster, but although, ideally, I would not buy a horse with this problem, I have actually had quite a few horses who did this and none ever actually lamed themselves.

Using brushing boots for schooling is a sensible precaution, and correct training and development can certainly improve the way in which the horse moves. With greater control over his actions he may even not knock himself at all.

A lot also depends on the age of the horse. Young horses who are still developing would tend to improve in front and behind so when looking at a horse assessment of his condition as well as his age and training could be helpful.

UNLEVEL

Uneven or unlevel steps can occur for two main reasons; a fault in the training or a problem such as lameness. This can be in the feet, the legs or other areas including the back and hips.

You should be suspicious of a horse that does not stand

foursquare, but continually rests the same leg, or, when at halt, steps back with one or (especially) both hind legs. When moving, the size of the horse's steps should be consistant. In particular, look for equal overtracking of the hind feet because this is often where an unlevelness will show most.

From behind, the hips should look level; one should not be lower than the other. Each hock should flex equally to the same height.

Look at each gait critically because some horses will be unlevel in walk but not in trot and so on. Beware of any sign of stringhalt (snatching upwards of one or both hind legs) because this would be marked severely in a dressage competition.

Some unlevelness is very slight, momentary or may wear off. If you have noticed it but still want to buy the horse, do ask your veterinary surgeon to investigate the problem for you when he examines him.

Unlevelness might be caused during training by the rider having allowed the horse to become one-sided or stiff. A knowledgeable rider could, after riding the horse for a short time, state whether or not he felt the fault *was* a training fault, although he might cover himself by advising a veterinary check as well.

IRREGULAR
Irregular steps occur when the rhythm changes for a few steps, or keeps changing as the horse alters his speed or impulsion.

Young horses may well be irregular in their trot because they will not have reached the stage of training where a speed is established in their minds. Similarly, their development and balance will not have reached a stage where they are able to maintain a set amount of impulsion, so they will constantly be losing or gaining it. As they become more balanced, better muscled and established in their knowledge, so the irregularities disappear.

Unlevelness and irregularity can be confused so, when

seeing a horse for the first time, look carefully and possibly take a knowledgeable person with you; they will know the difference and may also see something you might miss.

Canter

FLAT (LACKING SUSPENSION)

This is one problem that you can really do without if you have any choice in the matter. No real moment of suspension when all the legs are off the ground at the same time, will result in a variety of difficulties.

There will be a tendency for the horse to canter in a four-time beat instead of three-time which will lose many marks in competitions.

He will also find flying changes difficult because there will be no real moment for the change of lead to take place. Collection will be a problem because as the stride is shortened it may have even less suspension. Lateral work and pirouettes are often laboured or hurried because the horse cannot cover the ground during the moment he is in the air.

A lot can be done to improve bad canters by building up impulsion and gradually achieving more collection to make the horse 'jump', in the stride, but, because it is an effort, the horse will always try to revert to his original canter.

Having said all that, I have had horses who have won even at advanced standard with poor canters, but only after a lot of work to make them supple and obedient enabling them to pick up marks for other reasons.

FOUR-TIME

A four-beat canter can be caused by the horse having virtually no moment of suspension between the strides. He appears to leave a leg on the ground all the time and each leg is working separately giving an unattractive running gait.

Some horses have naturally flat canters which are hard to improve, but the chief cause of a four-time canter is lack of impulsion or energy. The immediate cure for this is to give the horse a kick and send him forwards whereupon the canter should instantly improve and have a recognisable moment of suspension.

Sometimes impulsion will be lost as the rider tries to collect the horse for some particular exercise and then as the canter loses height it can become four-time.

CHANGING BEHIND (DISUNITED)

I have found that quite a few people worry about this irritating habit because they believe that something is physically wrong with the horse. I say 'habit' deliberately as I have had to deal with this problem many times and have always found it to be caused by a stiffness which the unknowledgeable rider has allowed the horse to develop. There may be times when a disunited canter could be a problem for the veterinary surgeon, but I would be very surprised indeed if it could not be corrected very simply by better riding.

Horses of all types can develop this habit particularly in the corners of a school or arena, or in the transition from canter to trot, but Arabs do seem to be particularly prone to this problem.

Suppling exercises, especially shoulder-in and making the horse bend round the rider's inside leg, usually make him more able to hold the canter correctly on circles and in corners, but if the horse is very stiff, a firmer use of the outside rein and leg will help to hold the quarters and prevent the outside hind leg from going out, which allows the change behind.

In the transition from canter to trot the canter will need straightening by using the outside rein and leg more to control the side to which he will swing.

I have not found any permanent or recurring difficulty in correcting this fault.

47

CHANGING IN FRONT (DISUNITED)

This fault would not in my opinion be a habit in the same way as changing behind, but more a question of the horse saving his balance at a time when he is not getting much help from his rider!

9
Action

Dishing

When a horse dishes, either one or both front legs swing out to the side; the action comes from the lower leg (from the knee down) or just from the foot, or feet. It can be rather ugly and some people are horrified by the sight of it.

Unless the action is exaggerated, I do not worry about it all that much and it is not, or should not, be marked down in a dressage competition. I would not buy a mediocre horse with poor action but if he was otherwise talented, I might do so.

Pigeon Toes

The front feet of a pigeon-toed horse turn in towards each other. Improvement can sometimes be made by good shoeing but, often, pigeon-toed horses seem to trip over their own feet, and they seldom move very well. For these reasons, if I were offered a horse with this particularly unattractive action I would probably not buy him.

Moving Too Close

As mentioned previously, a horse which moves too close with either front or back legs is in danger of injuring itself,

49

but, in addition, there is an even stronger possibility that the legs may cross each other, i.e. plaiting.

As dressage requires that each hind leg shall follow in the track of the relevant foreleg, on straight lines and circles, any other action would prevent the horse from being successful.

If legs cross each other they are frequently accompanied by a swinging of the forehand and/or hindquarters; this is particularly detrimental because the horse will never be truly straight.

It could not be said that *all* horses which move close are not straight but think carefully before deciding to buy one with this action.

Daisy Cutting

This generally accepted term describes the action of the foreleg which comes forwards straight and close to the ground as if cutting the heads off the daisies with the toes.

Although it can look quite pretty and is desirable in some show horses and ponies it is not very suitable for dressage because any action where the joints do not flex is stiff or stilted.

Rounded Action

By this I mean a slightly rounded look to the foreleg as it is picked up and comes forward, with an elevated knee. This action usually accompanies a good lift from the shoulder giving scope to the stride and activity to the movement. The hind legs should also flex well at each joint.

Hackney Action

Some horses have the high-stepping leg action of the

Hackney horse, and a toned down version of this movement can be quite suitable for dressage providing it is not jerky or tense.

Ideal Action

The ideal movement for dressage should be smooth and easy looking, a pleasure to watch, with plenty of scope and freedom of the gaits, slightly rounded, with all the joints working energetically and effectively. The hind legs should propel the horse foward actively, working under the hindquarters giving height and energy to the stride. The forelegs should lift with the shoulder to allow maximum reach and ground coverage.

The feet should come to the ground with level tread and the four legs should match each other in action and not be exaggerated in front or lacking behind.

A complete eveness of stride combined with natural, or created, rhythm is essential, which should be so defined as to give a special quality or cadence, to the steps. This can only be achieved by regular steps and with good moments of suspension in trot and canter which have been derived from suppleness and submission and never tension.

10
Conformation and Appearance

The Head

SET OF HEAD ON TO NECK

I think is is very important that where the head joins the neck there is plenty of room for flexion; it is also more elegant. A horse with a fat neck at the join will have trouble flexing, and the neck will wrinkle in the throatlash area. There are many horses who do have difficulty owing to the set of the head, but this is no excuse for the horse not coming on the bit. Providing he accepts the aids willingly he can comply with his rider's wishes perfectly satisfactorily.

Riders should be careful, however, that in striving to achieve the flexion they require in this throat/neck area, they do not overdo it causing restriction of the windpipe.

APPEARANCE

There is no such thing as an ideal head for dressage but it is quite important that it is in proportion to the rest of the horse or it may look ugly. We all have our own ideas about the 'perfect' head, but this is of less importance than so many other things.

I do think that perhaps some colour on the head can be helpful in drawing attention to a horse because plain heads can be rather nondescript. A star or star and stripe down the centre of the face is quite attractive.

The Ears

LOP-EARED

The sort of ears which flop out to each side and sometimes to the front, can be quite endearing but they do not really create the right picture for a dressage horse. This picture is important and, because there is nothing you can do about lop ears, try to avoid buying a horse that has them.

LARGE

Some people think large ears are ugly, but I do not mind them and do not think that they necessarily detract from the overall picture.

CARRIED-BACK

There are a few horses, fortunately in the minority, who, when ridden, do not prick their ears; this gives an appearance of disinterest.

When I first met the problem I thought that the horse was bored, and if I gave him something more to think about or woke him by using different exercises, changes of gait and so on, the ears would prick. This was not so; it would seem that a horse with carried-back ears is simply more comfortable with his ears in that position, they are quite relaxed and he listens to the rider. Training the horse, therefore, is not a problem, the only problem is in the unsatisfactory picture these ears present.

I was once told by an eminent riding master that he had never discovered how to overcome this difficulty.

The Mouth

THE TONGUE

There can be a variety of problems with the horse's tongue, most of which are to do with evading the pressure of the bit.

Occasionally there can be a problem because of an injury or even a deformity at birth. In the former case, evasion can be overcome by better bitting, more sympathetic riding or more knowledgable training. In the latter case, if the tongue is damaged or deformed it may continue to be a problem.

Evasions by the tongue are generally manifested in four ways: the tongue coming over the bit, being drawn back, protruding out of the side of the mouth or being held between the teeth.

The first two, the tongue coming over the bit, or drawing back, may happen most of the time if the horse has learned that they relieve pressure, or they may happen momentarily in a transition or when the rider is asking for collection. They often occur when the horse is asked to do something he considers difficult.

These problems can be corrected by making sure that the snaffle, or bridoon if using a double bridle, fits well up into the corners of the mouth, and by fitting a flash or drop noseband to prevent the mouth from opening far enough for the horse to draw back his tongue and/or put it over the bit. Correct riding and retraining the horse to accept the aids better will also help prevent these problems.

Horses who have learned to hang their tongues out of the side of the mouth or hold it between their teeth are hard to correct. I have found that the only real answer is to retrain the horse to accept the aids, that is, to answer the driving aids from the legs which send impulsion to the hands which in turn must soften the mouth. If there is resistance in the horse's poll or jaw the rider cannot succeed.

If a horse is being worked correctly, lengthening and shortening within the gait will be employed, and these exercises together with suppling exercises keep the horse alert, paying attention to the rider, which helps to keep the tongue in the right place.

THE TEETH
Before buying a horse you will want to know how old he is. Even if the owner tells you the age, check this for yourself, and look at the condition of the teeth. Obviously, if you are having the horse vetted, these things will be ascertained for

you but there are some things you can check for yourself. For example, sometimes the horse has teeth missing, he may have had an injury or have a crooked or parrot mouth. It is important that the teeth meet in such a way that he can chew his food properly. Look for worn front teeth; this is a sign that the horse has been cribbing or windsucking.

Many faults and evasions are blamed on wolf teeth and, indeed, they can sometimes be a problem if they are in the way of the bit. They can be removed, but your veterinary surgeon will judge what is best for the horse.

Even if you cannot ascertain the exact age of the horse, it is quite simple to tell at least whether it is very young, middle-aged or old by the length of the teeth.

The Eyes

Good sight is, naturally, important so have the horse's eyes checked thoroughly by the veterinary surgeon.

I have, however, had several horses to train who had sight in only one eye, and have found that, for dressage, once they are trained it does not affect their performance. During training they sometimes resist moving into their blind slide, in lateral work, but once they know and accept the aids and trust their riders, they perform perfectly adequately.

There has always been prejudice against horses which show the whites of their eyes or have small eyes because they can give the horse a mean appearance. I feel this theory is a fallacy because I have known plenty of horses like this who have been kind and generous, and others with so-called 'big, generous' eyes who have been extremely ill-tempered. Nevertheless, it is possible to glean a great deal about a horse's nature by looking at his eyes.

The Neck

HIGH

A horse with a high neck and head carriage is preferable to one with a low neck and head carriage because, generally, these horses are not built on the forehand and, with correct use of the aids, they develop a 'round' shape more easily. I think they also have much more presence. The only disadvantage would be that a horse with this conformation might dislike working in a rounded outline, and it could take some time to build the muscles correctly along the crest, back and croup, particularly if the horse has been allowed to work above the bit and develop a muscular bulge on the under-neck.

LOW

Horses who have necks which dip in front of the withers and then tend to go straight out in front of the withers, have great difficulty in ever being able to arch the neck in front of the rider. This will give the impression of heaviness of the forehand; an unattractive picture, and not one you should have in mind for a dressage horse.

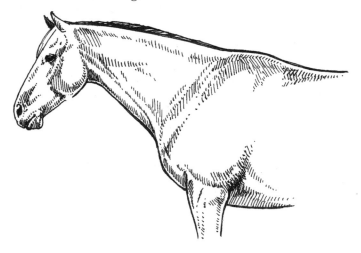

Low neck

Long neck

LONG

Most people find a long neck preferable to a short neck, but sometimes a horse with an exceptionally long neck can be difficult to train. As a novice the horse would only be corrected by the aids to a small degree and be allowed to keep his neck stretched forward. The difficulty arises when, as training progresses, the rider wishes to bring the horse together more and requires a greater degree of flexion at the poll.

To avoid the flexion, some horses, instead of bending correctly at the poll, will curl their neck round and downwards thus placing the poll lower than the rest of the neck when it should be the highest point. Many horses discover this is easier than working correctly, and it is an evasion that riders will find harder to correct with a long-necked horse than with a short-necked horse.

Building up the neck with both fat and muscle helps to disguise its length, especially if muscle can be developed on the crest, so a combination of clever feeding and correct riding can help this problem.

SHORT

A short-necked horse will, in addition, often have a badly set on head allowing very little space for flexion, thus making flexion difficult for him. Consequently he will not present a very good picture. Unless the rider is clever and able to keep the horse's nose well in front of the vertical, the neck, as the horse flexes and comes onto the bit, may appear even shorter than it is.

Even if the horse's conformation is correct, the rider may, when striving for collection, shorten the neck by overresisting with his hands. This also happens sometimes in extension if the horse is balancing on the rider's hands and is not able to stretch himself as required.

Should you be tempted by a horse with a beautiful stride but a short neck in proportion to the rest of him, do bear in mind that a horse's gaits can be made more attractive by developing perfect rhythm, but a glaring fault in the conformation can never be changed.

Short neck

58

Ewe neck

EWE

A so-called ewe neck describes one where the crest is concave rather than convex.

It is important to assess whether a horse's ewe neck stems from his natural conformation or whether he is simply in poor condition. It may also be that he has just been ridden incorrectly. It is not always easy to see which it is but, as a guide, I think if the dip is accompanied by a low neck it is probable that the conformation is bad and it is unlikely that it will be possible to change the shape.

On the other hand if the neck comes upwards from the dip there may be a chance that, with the correct work, the musculature can be improved.

An additional problem is that if the ewe-necked horse is made to work with his head in the correct position prior to building up the correct musculature, the dip will remain, and a build up of muscle on the underside of the neck will evolve which will look unattractive and be difficult to get rid of. Consequently most ewe-necked horses have to be ridden with their necks and heads low (not on the forehand) and as they learn to engage behind and round their backs the muscles in front of the withers will begin to develop and eventually the dip will go. Because the under-neck has been kept the correct shape by working with the neck low (in line with the withers), when the forehand is raised by the use of the quarters, the neck will arch from the withers and the dip will disappear.

I have had quite a number of horses who have started with bad necks but after a year or two have acquired crested, muscled necks. It can take some time especially if they have had a poor start with lack of feed or unknowledgable training, but the time and effort spent can be worth it in the end.

The Shoulders

STRAIGHT
A straight or upright shoulder will almost certainly affect the way the horse moves; it limits the distance that the front leg can stretch, and the amount he can lift the shoulder which helps provide suspension in the trot and canter. The horse may also be either uncomfortable or jarring to ride, or he may shuffle instead of really moving forwards.

It would be impossible to actually alter the natural stride of such horses, but any horse can be improved with systematic work and suppling exercises.

HEAVILY BUILT
Some horses are built in such a way that most of the weight is taken on the shoulders and forelegs. Because dressage training is all about transferring weight to the hindquarters to lighten the forehand, it is an aggravating problem to try to solve, and improvement may not be possible to a very high degree.

If the horse is co-operative and does not use his weight to obstruct the rider, some transference of the weight can be achieved by the use of half-halts. Suppling exercises, such as circles of varying sizes and shoulder-in, will also help to engage the quarters to aid better carrying power.

The Back

LONG
If you are contemplating buying a horse with a long back do bear in mind a couple of points.

First, if it is long in the back and lacking front it will look like that whatever you do, and will always make you look as if you are sitting on the shoulders! This is an especially unfortunate picture if the horse is also short in the leg as the impression will be that of a dachshund dog.

Some long-backed horses 'tail off' badly as well, accentuating the problem. Sometimes it helps if the horse carries a little extra weight, but it will not cure the problem. If the horse is only slightly long-backed but has a reasonable front, the use of a white saddle cloth to cover some of the offending area can improve the picture.

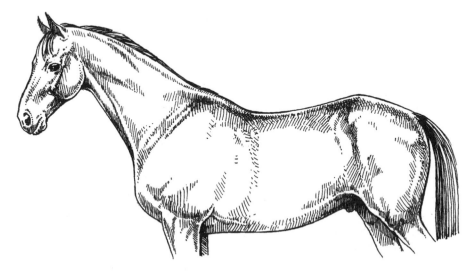

Long back

61

The second, perhaps even more vital, point is that long-backed horses do have more difficulty in tracking-up in walk and trot, and are sometimes physically unable to 'overtrack', as is required in walk.

Because of the distance between the quarters and the forehand there is also great difficulty in engaging the quarters adequately which is a problem when trying to collect the horse.

Unaccountably some long-backed horses piaffe exceptionally well but, as this is only a small proportion of the work required, I believe on the whole it is better to avoid them.

SHORT

An exceptionally short-backed horse may look better than one which is long-backed but there are problems peculiar to short backs.

Firstly, there is a very small area upon which to sit and, unless quite small and slight, the rider will appear to swamp the horse.

Secondly, because the 'motor' (hindquarters) is almost directly under the seat the stride action together with the impulsion tends to throw the rider out of the saddle. The rider can get used to this by developing more strength in the depth of his seat and thus become more secure.

Another problem is that, because of the short back, there is not much horse to 'wrap' round the inside leg of the rider for the lateral work, making the work a little harder than it would be if the back was a better length.

HOLLOW

A horse can have a hollow back for two main reasons: the fault may arise from incorrect training, i.e. if the horse has been allowed to carry his head too high for a long time and not been made to go on the aids properly, or it can be a skeletal fault resulting from injury or deformity.

It will be apparent when the cause is incorrect training because, when the horse is being ridden, he will tend to

Hollow back

come above the bit, causing his back to dip under the rider. The croup will almost certainly be high as well, in which case the hind legs will tend to thrust out behind the quarters rather than coming under them.

When the horse is assessed 'stripped' his back will actually look normal, although there will almost certainly be weakness because muscles which should have developed from him going correctly in a 'rounded' outline, will not have done so.

A skeletal problem will be quite obvious when you see the horse without the saddle because there will be a distinct deformity where the spine dips behind the withers. I have known one such horse who when saddled gave no impression of this fault at all and it never affected his work, and although I have not actually found this problem to cause lameness or real difficulty, I could not recommend anyone to take it on unless, perhaps, the horse was a gift!

ROACH

This is quite an ugly deformity; the spine between the withers and the croup arches upwards like a bow. It is also quite uncomfortable because you feel you are perched on top of the horse, with the forehand and quarters falling away at each end. Neither can it be comfortable for the horse because his back, which would normally swing up and down under the rider, tends to be rigid.

Apart from the appearance, I have found the performance to be affected as well and therefore would rule out buying a horse with this problem.

Roach back

COLD

A cold-backed horse, when saddled, girthed-up or mounted, tends to either sink in the back or arch the back very tensely.

If the back sinks, it may be wise to check that there is nothing wrong with the saddle, and perhaps seek veterinary advice because there may be an internal problem.

Some horses sink because they have been mounted badly. If the rider drags on the saddle, the withers or the spine can become bruised, or if he drops unsympathetically onto the horse's back, instead of sitting down carefully, the horse will anticipate the pain and try to take his back away.

If the back is arched in protest against something, it is, very often, the girth and I would suggest that once again the saddle is checked, but it is more likely that the rider will have put the saddle on the horse roughly, or girthed-up too tightly, too quickly.

There are a few horses who go through life disliking the feel of the girth, but provided owners are sympathetic and girth-up slowly this should not be a problem. There may be a few horses who react badly however careful you are, but in these cases I have always found that a piece of elastic inserted below the buckles overcomes the difficulty by providing a little more give in the girth.

The Withers

HIGH
I do not think that I have come across any training problems relating to high withers, apart from having to find a saddle which will fit! This can be a problem, and quite often you have to resort to a saddle with a cut-back head. This is, however, perfectly satisfactory if you are comfortable in this type of saddle.

When contemplating buying a horse with high withers it might be wise to, first, try a saddle on him in which you know you are comfortable.

LOW
Low or flat withers can cause some training difficulties because if the saddle continually rides forward it will impede the action of the horse's shoulders and put the rider

in front of the centre of gravity. However, it is not an insoluble problem because there is a useful piece of equipment called a fore-girth which is rather like an arch roller and fits in front of the saddle to keep it back in position.

The Quarters

CROUP-HIGH

We talk about horses being croup-high in competitions when they are insufficiently engaged behind and, instead of lowering their quarters, they evade by resisting the rider and stiffening their backs and quarters.

If a horse has learned to evade in this way it can be quite difficult to get him to work properly because he will have to be taught to respect the rider's leg aids and made to go forwards. The rider may be faced with resentment because the horse is being made to alter his way of going, which can take time to achieve. As the horse will be unable to perform advanced dressage movements until he learns to lower his quarters, it is very important that this can be put right.

Some horses however are actually built higher behind than in front, which can be seen clearly if the horse is made to stand on level ground. It should not be said that it is impossible for such horses to do advanced work, I have known several who have, but it is very much more difficult for the horse and requires an extremely skilful rider.

I could not recommend any horse with this problem to an average rider and, in any case, it is not fair to the horse.

NARROW

If the actual structure of the horse's quarters is narrow, then almost certainly the back legs will be close together with the possibility of the horse knocking himself when working. As dressage training, especially at advanced level, is very tough on the quarters they need the maximum possible strength. Narrowness would point towards weakness, so I would not wish to buy a horse like this.

Lack of fitness or condition can make a horse *look* narrow in his quarters so study the horse carefully to see whether you think it is his build or just a matter of feeding.

The Hips

APPEARANCE OF HIPS
As the hindquarters have to do so much of the work it is important that they are strong. Evenness of the hips (seen from behind) is an important factor; anything which does not seem quite equal should be viewed with suspicion.

Hips sometimes stick out in a rather unattractive fashion but this can be due to the horse's breeding, (the more common types tend to be like this) or it can be due to lack of condition. You will need to study the frame carefully before deciding which it is.

From a training point of view I have not found that protruding hips have a detrimental effect, just that from behind they are not as aesthetically pleasing as hips which do not.

UNLEVEL OR DROPPED
It is very important when making a purchase that you stand behind the horse (well back in case it kicks!) to study the evenness of the hips.

There are horses who have one hip lower than the other, either from injury or deformity, and quite often the muscles between the hip and the croup will be unevenly developed because of this. Although he may not be lame or even unlevel in his stride I think it would be most unwise to buy a horse with this problem. You could well find that as a horse comes under the pressures of training he will become unlevel.

I did once have a horse with the point of one hip knocked

off through injury. The actual hips were not affected and the horse worked perfectly satisfactorily all his life, but this is not the same as having a dropped hip.

The Tail

LOW
It is unfortunate if a horse has a low-set tail because, on the whole, it is unattractive, and they find difficulty 'carrying' the tail which spoils the look of the hindquarters.

The tail can, of course, be nicely pulled and cared for, and if everything else about the horse was exceptional, a low-set tail could be tolerated if there was no other choice.

THICK
Some of the more common types of horse do have very thick rather carthorsey tails. I would not be put off by this, however, because, although the tail will be a job to pull and will need a lot of attention, it can be made to look quite nice.

If part of the tail gets caught between the back legs as the horse works, thinning the tail is recommended, because, if left thick, it will detract from the overall picture and distract the judge's attention.

LENGTH
A long tail can of course be trimmed to the desired length but occasionally, for one reason or another, a horse will have a short wispy tail. This is a minor problem if the horse is good at his job, but if the tail does not grow it can look unattractive and, as with a thick tail, spoils what should be an attractive picture.

HELD TO ONE SIDE
I would not like to be dogmatic about the reason for this happening because some breeds have a natural tendency to carry their tails this way, but quite often it denotes a stiffness or tension along the back muscles which lead to the

tail and, instead of the tail swinging in a relaxed way, it is held rigidly to one side. The cause may be a muscular or skeletal injury and, if so, could be virtually impossible to erase.

I have corrected the problem with a number of horses simply by making them more supple, so, although I would not particularly want to buy a horse with a one-sided tail, I might if everything else was exactly what I wanted.

Although it could not be specifically marked down in a competition the judge would view it with suspicion and be inclined to be less generous than with a horse with a central tail carriage.

The Knees

TIED-IN BELOW THE KNEE
If the horse is tied-in below the knee, the leg is at its narrowest and therefore weakest at that point.

Joints suffer a great deal of wear and tear and need to be well supported by the surrounding area; support that, for a knee joint, is lacking from a leg that is tied-in below the knee.

Action is not affected by this conformation fault so, from a training point of view, it is not a disaster, but of course with any weakness there could be lameness which would be a disaster, especially if a lot of work had gone into the horse's training.

OVER AT THE KNEE
I am not sure of the cause of this fault, but standing over at the knee is something that occurs quite a lot in Thoroughbreds; some of them stand with their knees well forward from the rest of the leg, and the legs may tremble quite violently in some cases.

In an ideal situation I would not choose a horse with this fault, however I have trained a great number of horses who were over at the knee, none of whom was lame and all worked well into old age.

Being over at the knee should not, therefore, be detrimental to a horse's training, neither should it affect the judging of the horse in competition.

BACK AT THE KNEE

When a horse who is back at the knee is viewed from the side, instead of the front leg coming out of the shoulder and going straight to the ground, the impression is of the leg bowing backwards. This, in my opinion, is a weakness because the tendon is stretched more than it should be and, although the horse may never go lame, it is something to consider carefully.

If you were going to show the horse it would be classed as a conformation fault but if the horse is sound it would not particularly affect dressage training or action.

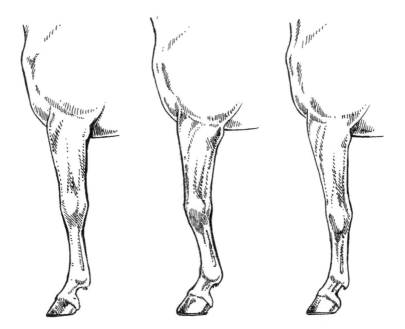

Tied-in below the knee (left);
over at the knee (centre); back at the knee (right).

The Second Thigh

This being the part of the leg between the hock and the stifle, it is important that it is strong. Quite a few horses are simply unmuscled in this area which, if the horse is young, is probably not a problem. In the case of an older horse however it is more worrying because it means that there could actually be a weakness.

Even if you think that the horse's muscle development has been retarded by bad riding it could be that it is too late to make a sufficient change.

I would seriously consider not buying a horse whose second thigh is rather light in proportion to the rest of the body because, even if the thigh itself never caused a problem, it could put strain upon the remainder of the leg.

The Hind Legs

STRAIGHT HIND LEGS

I think it is a tremendous disadvantage for a horse to have a straight hind leg, i.e. when he is standing still the arch from the quarters to the point of hock is very shallow, and when on the move the hock joint bends very little. Horses with this conformation generally find it easier to swing the leg forward with minimum effort, making it hard to get them to really work but, worst of all, it makes them look as if they are inactive. This, from a competition point of view, is disastrous because many marks are lost if the horse is lacking activity.

Straight back legs are not a physical hindrance to training and these horses can still be trained to Grand Prix standard, but they are an obvious disadvantage if the judges are going to mark you down throughout the horse's career because he appears inactive.

SICKLE HOCKS

Sickle hocks have an exaggerated curve from the quarters to

the point of the hock and then, below the hock, the leg is angled forwards so that the cannon bone is not straight to the ground.

In some respects these two faults create a false impression. First, the arch from the quarters to the point of hock can flex quite well making the horse appear active. Second, the forward angles of the lower part of the legs give the impression that the horse is working well with his hind legs under the body, all of which judges will like!

Up to a point this is all very well because some riders will say that anything that gains marks in competitions has to be good. I would agree, but my one worry would be that, because the leg is technically built incorrectly, there will at some time be stress which may cause lameness.

COW HOCKS

This term describes hocks which, at the point of hock, almost touch each other, and the horse's toes turn outwards. Clearly, if the legs are not straight they will be weaker than straight legs and, because of the work they have to do, this is a disadvantage.

Training cannot alter what is a conformation defect, but there are plenty of horses with cow hocks who perform well.

All I can say is that cow hocks are not something to take on if they can be avoided.

WIDE HIND LEGS

Wide hind legs are set on to the quarters in such a way that the horse moves with his back legs going to the side instead of under his body. This wide-behind action is rather like a duck waddling which, on a duck, is quite appealing, but on a horse it is singularly unattractive.

Some horses will go wide behind owing to incorrect training, having been allowed to get on the forehand and never having had the quarters properly engaged. Others will use this particular problem to evade collection by stiffening their backs so that the back legs go even wider making it impossible for the rider to engage the quarters correctly. Invariably I have found that, although the rider can be blamed to some extent, the horse probably tends to do this anyway.

A knowledgable rider would be able to correct a training fault but if the horse goes wide behind when he is running loose, then I would not buy him.

BUILT OUT HIND LEGS

The more the hind legs are set underneath the hindquarters the better, because they will be able to engage more easily and come under the body in order to 'carry' the horse and lighten the forehand.

If, when the horse is at halt, the hind legs are naturally angled backwards from the hindquarters they are said to be built out behind. If this is so, apart from the difficulty in obtaining engagement, the loins of the horse will be stretched and forced to work in a way which could cause strain. The actual effort the horse will have to make to propel himself forwards will be greater if he is continually thrusting himself forwards instead of lifting, which will be the case if the hind legs are under the body.

Without engagement the horse's balance will never be good, he may well drag himself along by his forehand, and, in addition, go wide behind in his effort.

DRAGGING TOES

This problem is made apparent by the wear of the toes of the hind shoes. Some horses only drag one toe while others drag both equally.

Although it is not desirable to have a horse which does either, I would prefer the one who drags both hind toes, because if he only drags one this points to some trouble with that particular hind leg which the other does not show.

Some horses are simply idle and need waking up, and some can be improved by making them work more actively in a rounded outline, because hollowness or being above the bit can cause this problem. Unfortunately there are a few horses who, however well they are ridden, continue to drag their toes. I think in most cases lack of flexion of the joints is the reason as well as lack of stride suspension.

Sadly, these horses give themselves away in competitions because their back feet leave a little furrow behind them which informs the judge of their inactivity.

WOBBLY HOCKS
When the horse walks or trots away from you one or both hocks screw outwards. It is pretty unsightly and you would certainly think that it must be a weakness.

I have known quite a few horses with wobbly hocks and have not ever seen them lame, but, if a horse I was thinking of buying had the problem, I would not take the risk.

I believe it is natural to a horse and nothing to do with bad training, therefore nothing specific can be done and it is impossible to disguise.

The Feet

We all know the old saying 'no foot, no horse', and there are a great many things in the foot that can cause lameness so it is most important that they are sound. They should be a sensible size for the weight and height of the horse, nice and round in shape and not upright or boxy.

Some foreign horses tend to be more upright than the British breeds but, because they are bred that way, it is not necessarily a fault.

Flat feet very often give trouble as do contracted heels, and an odd foot (one which is quite different from the other three) would be looked upon with suspicion.

I would try not to buy a horse with large feet as they do tend to detract from the elegance desired in dressage competitions, but on the other hand he can get you through bad going better than a horse with smaller feet.

Always have the feet inspected by a vet before buying a horse.

FLAT FEET

I think it is most important that you do not choose a horse with flat feet, i.e. soles too close to the ground. Problems such as hard ground causing bruising, greater sensitivity to sharp stones, hooves which spread and crack etc., are more common to horses with flat feet.

Sometimes, because the angle of the sole does not sufficiently support the structure, internal damage and alterations to the angle of the bones of the foot can occur.

It may be disappointing to rule out a beautiful horse because he has flat feet, but it could save you heartache later.

11
The Skeletal Frame

Narrow Frame

I must admit that whenever I seen an overnarrowly built horse coming up the centre line at the beginning of a test, I am slightly put off, and although I would go on to judge the training, that important first impression has been made!

There are practical difficulties as well, and my main objection as a rider is that it can be exceedingly difficult to get your legs on the horse because his barrel disappears at the point where you want to make contact.

Some horses are only narrow because they are young, underfed, undeveloped or undermuscled but if it is because of their frame then, of course, nothing can be done.

The front legs of a narrow horse may be too close together causing not only brushing or speedy-cutting but also plaiting, i.e. crossing one foreleg in front of the other. Plaiting can also be a fault of well-built horses as a result of poor training but, with a narrow-framed horse, you are starting with a handicap.

Similarly the hind legs can, if too close together, damage each other and generally lack strength.

Despite the possibility of these problems, there is nothing to say that a narrow horse cannot be trained as well as any other, so if you already own one and are quite happy with him do not be put off by my remarks!

Wide Frame

It is rather difficult to define 'wide' as there could be varying degrees of width, some of which would suit one section of riders, and some would overstretch others and be decidedly uncomfortable.

I think it would be fair to say that riders with short thighs are also going to have a lot of difficulty getting their legs round the horse, and this will affect their position and security in the saddle. Without this correct positioning and security a rider will have a problem creating sufficient impulsion and will therefore be ineffective.

A wide frame does not present training problems providing the rider fits the horse.

Twisted Chassis

When looking at a horse for the first time most people will look at it from the side to see if the animal is in proportion, then walk round it to view him from the front and from behind.

Some structural problems are not apparent until the horse is on the move so it will be important to watch him walk and trot towards you and away from you. Thus, you should be able to observe any fault which will be shown up by the hind legs not following in the tracks of the forelegs. For example, the quarters may well be held to one side, or the steps may not be even, and one side of the horse may look lower than the other.

Whatever the fault, it may well have been caused by the horse having had a fall or an accident at some time, or he may, of course, have been born like it.

It is extremely unlikely that anything can be done for a horse with a twisted chassis, but only a veterinary surgeon can really advise you.

Stiffness and Fused Vertebrae

Nearly all horses which have been ridden are stiff because riders make them so. They may be stiff laterally or horizontally, or both, and will very likely be more stiff on one side than the other.

Horses, like humans, are born a little one-sided, but will also have other reasons for being stiff. They may have used the muscles on one side of their body more than the other and therefore find it difficult to flex the spine easily to both left and right. They may have arthritis in their backs, hips or other joints, and although arthritis does not make them permanently lame, the horse needs time to loosen the joints before hard work begins.

Sometimes bones fuse together to strengthen a weak area, for example vertebrae fusing in the spine, or they may do so as the result of injury from a fall.

Assessing the reason needs knowledge, both to determine the cause and then to decide whether there is anything that can be done and if it is worth the time and expense.

Retraining a horse from scratch by starting with simple exercises and building up to more difficult ones over a period of time may stretch and supple stiff muscles. This could be worthwhile if it is a good horse and not too old.

In the case of arthritis or fusions, a veterinary surgeon will tell you whether the horse has a future in dressage but, like all athletes, agility is vital to performance.

Bone

When people talk about good bone, they mean a good diameter of bone immediately below the knee or hock. Good bone is very important; it gives the strength which is vital for a long working life, and of course supports the horse's structure.

12
Physiology

Herring-gutted

This describes a lean, weedy-bodied horse with flat sides, and a bottom line which goes upwards sharply from the girth towards the quarters. I find it particularly unattractive and would certainly not buy a horse like this.

Sometimes horses which come out of racing are lean and very fit and may give the impression of being herring-gutted, but when they fill out they will have a better shape.

It may not be easy to tell the difference between a lean horse and a herring-gutted horse if you are inexperienced, but one guide is to look at the proportions of the belly in comparison to the rest of the horse to try to assess whether it looks 'light' or 'pinched'. Look also at the springing of the ribs, that is, how they come out of the backbone. If they come out to the side and are rounded, the horse may just be lean and should be all right, but if they drop straight from the spine to a more perpendicular position, the horse is bound to be flat sided.

Another problem is that whatever saddle you choose, because of the angle at which the belly goes upwards from the girth, the saddle will almost certainly slip back. A breast plate will hold the saddle in place and is allowed in competition, but it can still be a nuisance.

79

Potbellied

A potbelly does not, aesthetically, add to the overall picture the horse presents. The belly sags owing to poor nutrition, either from overfeeding or underfeeding, lack of exercise or possibly because the animal has had a foal. Whatever the cause, with the correct food and work, a pot-belly can be eliminated.

Splints

If a horse has a splint (a bony swelling between the splint bone and cannon bone) it may be that the extra bone has grown because the leg has had a knock, or it could be that the area has a tendency to be weak and the bone has grown to support it.

The quality of the horse's performance will depend upon the positioning of the splint. If it occurs very close to, or adjoining, a joint it could interfere with the horse's action and even make him lame, although I have owned horses with splints by the knee who remained sound. Small splints seldom seem to give trouble, especially when fully formed, unless they are too close to a tendon.

If the horse is not lame I have always ignored them. They are sometimes unsightly but, unless you are showing, you can learn to live with them. If they do cause trouble they can be removed surgically, but be guided by a veterinary surgeon on this matter.

Curbs

I would not buy a horse with curbs (ligament strains in the hock area) because I feel that the hocks are such a vital part of the horse, particularly for dressage, that I would rather not take the risk.

However, I have known horses with curbs pass a

veterinary inspection as fit for hard work, and some who have never been lame in spite of them, even in old age.

Certainly if anyone was contemplating buying a horse with this problem, the sensible thing to do would be to take veterinary advice.

Windgalls

Windgalls are soft swellings which occur above and around the fetlock joint. They are caused by wear and tear and, although unattractive to look at, cause no harm.

Keeping the horse's legs bandaged with woollen bandages while he's in the stable takes the windgalls down, and they will remain down for the duration of exercise.

Veterinary advice should be sought if you are considering buying a horse with pronounced windgalls because they may be an indication of undue wear and tear and even if they give no trouble themselves, the fetlocks may have suffered from the strain.

13
Habits and Vices

Under Saddle

REARING

When a horse reacts to something it does not want to do by rearing. it is a serious and dangerous resistance that is not easily corrected.

There are a few people who may be able to cure this nasty habit but once a horse has learned that he can blackmail his rider in this fashion he will, I venture to say, *never* forget it.

Do not be bamboozled by people who are trying to sell you a horse who 'only rears a little', or 'only when he sees a plough in a field'!

Always see the owner ride the horse first before you get on him and if there are any signs of rearing or real napping, do not get on but extract yourself as quickly as possible.

BUCKING

There are very few horses who buck as a resistance, or even to get their riders off deliberately, it is generally a purely natural expression of exuberance which, if done while ridden, can, nonetheless, indeed unship the rider!

With training, horses learn to curb this playful desire and buck only when turned loose. I believe that they need this freedom sometimes just as we need to relieve our own emotions.

Sometimes mistaken for bucking is a humping of the back which does involve the back feet just leaving the ground, but this is entirely different, being a distinct anti-reaction to a rider's leg aids, and is classed as napping. It has to be dealt with immediately and firmly with the use of a whip so that the horse is left in no doubt that this is unsociable behaviour and he will not be allowed to get away with it.

Like all forms of napping, the longer the horse is allowed to pursue his resistance to his rider's wishes the harder it will be to correct, so you are doing the horse and yourself a favour by overcoming it as quickly as possible.

Some horses can be really 'piggy' and if you feel you are getting nowhere with a horse, take him to someone more knowledgable who will soon deal with the problem.

NAPPING

Any form of resistance by the horse against the rider's aids is classed as napping, or the beginning of it, and should be eliminated as quickly as possible. It is no good being soft and sentimental!

Horses are basically owned for their riders' pleasure. Some are sadly misused but many lead a pampered life and should, therefore, reasonably be expected to do as they are told, in fact, they even prefer it once they understand the routine.

It would certainly be preferable not to buy a nappy horse because a good deal of time-consuming retraining will have to take place and this needs experience. A novice rider will not have the knowledge to correct a horse with too many naughty tricks.

If you have ridden for a number of years you will probably be able to deal with the problem and many a nappy horse has been turned into a champion by teaching it obedience through systematic training. Certainly it would be tempting to take on a retraining job if the horse was exceptional in his looks and gaits.

Some horses become nappy because their riders ask too much of them too soon before they are physically able, or can comprehend the request. Consequently, they become stiff, one-sided or dead in the mouth. Others may have been punished long after the event. Horses have wonderful memories but they do not have the capacity for logical thought, so if the humans, who are supposed to have the brain, do not use their powers of thought sensibly, horses may become confused and resistance will follow.

Training unspoilt horses is difficult enough but retraining a spoilt one, although fascinating and a great challenge, requires patience, determination and understanding.

BOLTING
I think that there are very few horses who really bolt because this means that they run in a blind panic, not seeing anything in their way and careering over or through everything. A true bolter is a very frightening and dangerous horse to ride.

Some horses are classed as bolters when they are simply untrained, have no mouth and are therefore unstoppable. This is caused by human stupidity and a lack of knowledge of how to teach a horse to answer the aids.

If such a thing happens to you I suggest you go back to the drawing board and check up on your riding and training knowledge.

If you are trying a horse who appears to have no brakes, ask very little of him, do not put yourself in danger and, if you decide to buy him, plan to take him back to square one when you get him home.

SHYING
The shying of a young horse who has been frightened by something he has not seen before is quite acceptable, but if an older horse does it to evade the rider's request, he is probably simply being naughty and needs discipline.

There are also those horses who spook pretending to be terrified of all manner of everyday sights, sounds and smells. A very firm line has to be taken with these cheeky animals, and once they realise their rider will not put up with their pranks, they will settle down and work.

Shying is a frustrating problem because all you have

recourse to is making the horse respond to and respect the aids, but obedience does evolve from this eventually.

Occasionally shying can be due to an eye defect, so if the shying persists, ask your veterinary surgeon to give the horse a check up.

In the Stable

WEAVING

Weaving originates from boredom or tension, the horse swings his head from side to side over the stable door or behind it if it is barred. In violent cases, the horse will throw itself from one forefoot to the other ceaselessly.

It is bad for the horse (in some cases the horse will lose weight), exceedingly irritating to watch, and other horses might pick up the habit.

A weaving grille attached to the top door prevents many horses from weaving and some only do it at certain times, when waiting for food for example, or while another horse is being taken away from the stable.

I have owned weavers and have found that with a good routine of feed and exercise, and a weaving grille, the problem can be alleviated, in some cases it almost stops. A horse with this habit would have to be exceptional in other ways for me to buy him, and it should certainly reduce the price!

WINDSUCKING

This is one habit that I cannot bear and I would never buy a horse, however gifted, that was affected in this way.

A confirmed windsucker gulps down air constantly in a frenzied fashion. The noise they make is horrible, sometimes they lose weight and the front teeth may become worn if they windsuck by catching hold of a fence or stable door. It is another habit that might be picked up by other horses.

A windsucking collar is a prevention rather than a cure

and sometimes has to be worn fairly tight which is unpleasant for the horse.

By law a vendor should inform you if his horse has this habit but if he does not you can return the horse and have your money refunded. Try not to put yourself in this situation; watch the horse in his stable and look for evidence of teeth marks on any piece of wood or protruding objects. If you find them, do not buy him.

CRIBBING

This habit can either be a serious or a minor problem, and often depends on the material of which the stable is made. If it is built of brick or block and render, and has a metal strip attached to the top of the door, there is very little chance for the horse to crib (chew). If, on the other hand, there is a good deal of woodwork the horse will happily gnaw his way through it probably contracting the habit of windsucking as well.

If he does not have the chance to chew on anything his attempts will be defeated in which case to own a cribber is not a disaster, but there is always the chance that windsucking will become an additional problem.

Any horse with a stable vice is a hazard and not to be taken on without a good deal of thought and knowledge of what it entails.

14
Difficulties with Loading into Lorries or Trailers

Unfortunately, owing to our incompetence, horses are often difficult to load into the various forms of transport we wish to use, or they are frightened by bad drivers. The driver of a vehicle will know where he is going next, or should do, but the unfortunate horse does not. He needs time to adjust his balance so unless speed is reduced gradually and he is given time to make alterations he will quite likely be thrown around or even fall down. It is not then surprising that he does not subsequently wish to load!

Drivers really must use some commonsense and try to imagine what it is like in a trailer. Although it is illegal to travel in one on the highway, it will do everyone some good to try standing up in a moving trailer or lorry to see what it is like.

If a young horse is loaded thoughtfully with patience, and given plenty of room by moving partitions over etc. he should not be worried, but if he is expected to scramble up a steep slippery ramp into a narrow dark area hitting his hips on the way in, he will not be keen next time.

Some older horses become crafty and stubbornly 'plant' themselves at the bottom of the ramp. A lunge rein attached to one side of the vehicle, brought round the horse just above his hocks and held by someone on the other side often encourages them to go in. Some horses only have to be shown the lunge rein as a threat and they walk straight in!

If you have a consistently difficult horse I would still advocate the lunge rein idea but possibly with two people and two lunge reins so that they can be crossed behind the horse and the horse 'levered' into the vehicle. If he should swing his quarters a whip may be used to keep him straight.

The person leading a difficult horse should lead in a bridle not a headcollar so that he cannot pull away, and in cases where the horse keeps getting his head up or rears, a standing martingale attached to the noseband and a roller helps to overcome this problem.

Another method is to long-rein the horse in but that, of course, requires someone capable of long-reining in the first place.

It is not always easy to assess whether the horse is frightened or stubborn but usually you can tell by the look in his eye, his general manner and attitude.

When purchasing a horse it is a good idea to ask whether the horse has travelled, in what and how much, and, if possible, see him loaded. Then, if he subsequently becomes a bad traveller or difficult to load, you know you must ask yourself when and why he changed. If you find the answer, you will know which way to tackle the problem to correct it.

15
General Handling

When looking at a prospective purchase, watch how the animal behaves when he is tacked up, taken away from the stable and mounted. Check his general attitude and the way he reacts to you; when you run your hand over his back and quarters does he snap or kick? Will he allow his feet to be picked up easily?

While you try this, see if he has been shod recently. If his feet and shoes are neglected he might be difficult with the farrier. You can also see if the shoes are worn unevenly, and whether care has been taken of the all important frog.

Ask if he has been clipped before. If he is six or older and has not there could be a problem. Look at the mane and tail to see if they have been pulled. A scruffy appearance may not merely mean that the owner has not had the time even if that is what he tells you. If he assures you that the horse is as good as gold, ask him to give a brief demonstration.

16
Trying a Strange Horse

There are a few important points to remember when you go to try any horse.
1. See him in the stable stripped to assess his nature and whether he weaves, cribs etc.
2. Have him 'stood up' for you in the yard, again, without his tack, to look at the conformation.
3. See him 'run up' and look at him from each side, from the front and behind to see if he moves straight.
4. Watch him being tacked up to see his reaction.
5. Always see the owner or someone connected to the owner ride him first and do not accept any excuses for them not doing so.
6. Wear a hard hat.
7. If possible see him loose in an enclosed area to see the natural action.
8. Ask about travelling, his behaviour with the farrier, whether he has any vices, what he is like in traffic and what injections he has had, flu, tetanus etc.
9. Finally, look at him again really critically and ask yourself whether he matches up to the picture of your ideal dressage horse, in what respects does he differ and do these points matter a lot or not much.

It is hardly ever possible to achieve your ideal but it is also easy to make a mistake just because he has beautiful eyes, a pretty head, a lovely nature and is your favourite colour.

17
Condition, Fitness and Turnout

Condition and Fitness

It can be pretty difficult, unless you are good at seeing the true structure of the horse, to visualise how one in poor condition would look when in good condition. I have been amazed so often at how horses can alter as they put on weight and muscle up.

Necks in particular can change dramatically in shape, quarters strengthen and the substance of the body is far greater than you would have thought possible. Instead of sitting on a narrow razor blade with your legs dangling round the belly, your legs will have something to take hold of as the horse's back broadens and his flanks widen.

The coat also improves; initially dull and harsh, it will soon start to feel smooth and have a shine even without being groomed.

As the horse is worked in the correct way systematically over a period of time, he develops the muscles he needs for dressage competition. His work will vary according to his age and temperament and, probably, his owner, because everyone has their own ideas on fitness, but the aim will be to get him fit enough to sustain energy for about an hour's riding in at a show plus the actual test, which although of relatively short duration, is very stressful in its concentrated form.

Not only is it much easier for the horse to perform well if he is fit, but it will be easier for the rider (who must also be fit) because the horse's energy will not run out during the test and he will still be willing. There is nothing more panic making than being half way through an advanced test and finding that the horse's impulsion is gradually fading away.

A horse in good condition, well-covered, round and shining will create a far better picture to a judge than one which is not, even if the training is just as good, and although it is the training that is being judged, there is little doubt that judges, being human, are impressed by a nice picture.

Turnout

Turnout is equally as important as condition and fitness. Good grooming, a nicely pulled tail and neat plaits complement yourself and the horse and are a mark of respect for the judge to whom you are presenting yourself.

It shows that you bother, which indicates a standard of care that suggests a probable dedication to training as well. It is surprising how slapdash turnout often accompanies a shoddy performance.

18
Choice of Sex for a Dressage Horse

Do you choose a mare, gelding or stallion? Naturally there will be those who are biased for or against one or other depending on their experience. In fact it may only be possible to decide which to have if you have ridden or tried to train one of each to find out which suits you.

I believe that all three can be equally good but that stallions should not be taken on by the inexperienced because they can soon get out of hand and can then be a real problem to correct.

Geldings can lack the sparkle of an entire, but are often fairly submissive to their rider's wishes and therefore may be easier to train.

Mares being a direct counterpart to the stallion show similar strong characteristics but when conquered are often generous and have a lot of stamina. There are those who can be a problem when ovulating but on the whole I have found them to be a small minority, and mares I have owned have performed as well or better than the males.

Whatever you take on you will need to fully understand that particular horse and be able to cope with his or her psychological and physical problems.

19
Finance

Always the great question is what to spend on the horse you want to train. Whether you have a lot of money or very little it is not easy to decide, although of course if money is no object there are many more options.

Some people will prefer to train their own horses, even if they are not all that experienced and I believe this to be the best way to learn, although expert advice will probably be required. Others will want to buy a school master, an older horse who can teach them. I have nothing against this idea but good ones are hard to find and will cost a lot of money.

There are those who feel that the best dressage prospects are to be found abroad; Dutch and German warmbloods are popular. Certainly these horses will have been given a good basic groundwork, will probably have done a canter change of leg and given a start in piaffe and/or passage.

Do bear in mind, however, that no-one sells an Olympic-standard horse if he thinks he has one (unless a fortune is being offered) and you might therefore still find yourself with a second rater, not a champion.

To afford good material is going to cost a lot of money nowadays but there are horses around who can do the job (sometimes the owners do not even realise what they have) and they are not all that expensive.

The important thing is to learn to train well because many a lesser animal can do surprisingly well if his training is correct.

Conclusion

Clearly, however perfect the horse you buy or own is in conformation, temperament and action, it still has to be ridden and trained for the job. I am sorry to say that I think there are far too many riders who, having probably spent a good deal of money on their choice of horse, seem to believe that they are now set to win, even though their own knowledge or ability may be quite limited.

How often do the professionals get asked to, 'take my horse for schooling to sort out his problems', not 'take me as a rider and sort out my problems'!

There is often far too much blame given to the horse for failure, when he, poor devil, is doing his utmost with a most inadequate or unfeeling rider. We talk a lot about disciplining the horse; very important, I agree, but what about the supreme dedication and self-discipline which the rider needs if he is to succeed.

Riding is very hard work and especially so in dressage where the rider has the complete responsibility for instructing the horse on his next move.

I would say that all horses, unless they have a serious conformation defect, can go quite nicely if ridden properly, and the better the horse, theoretically, the better he can go, but only if our own effort in learning and application permits.

You may have formed an opinion from the preceding pages that really it is a waste of time training anything bar the 'ideal', but this is not necessarily so, and is, in any case, impractical. If you own, or have just bought, a narrow, pigeon-toed horse which moves close behind and dishes as well do not despair because he can give you a lot of pleasure and satisfaction, and could still possibly be a winner!